"I Will Be Your God"

An Easy Introduction to
THE COVENANT OF GRACE

"I Will Be Your God"

An Easy Introduction to THE COVENANT OF GRACE

by Wes Bredenhof

Published by the
Inter-League Publication Board
Box 445 Fergus Ontario
Canada N1M 3E2

"I Will Be Your God" – An Easy Introduction to the Covenant of Grace
By Wes Bredenhof

Copyright © I.L.P.B. 2015

All Scripture quotations in this book are taken from the English Standard Version, unless otherwise noted.

All references to creeds, confessions and liturgical forms are to those found in the Book of Praise: Anglo-Genevan Psalter, 2014.

All rights reserved. No part of this publication may be reproduced, stored in a retrieval system, or transmitted in any form, or by any means, electronic, mechanical, photocopying, recording or otherwise, without prior written permission of the publisher.

Library and Archives Canada Cataloguing in Publication

Bredenhof, Wes, 1973-, author
    "I will be your God" : an easy introduction to the covenant of grace
/ Wes Bredenhof.

ISBN 978-0-88666-097-0 (paperback)

    1. Covenant theology. 2. Covenants--Religious aspects--Reformed Church. 3. Christian life--Reformed authors. I. Title.

BT155.B74 2015   231.7'6   C2015-904605-X

Cover design and Photography: John Vanveen

Published by the I.L.P.B.
Box 445, Fergus, Ontario
Canada N1M 3E2
www.ilpb.ca

ISBN-13 978-0-88666-097-0

Table of Contents

Preface	6
Chapter 1 – Introducing the Big Idea	8
Chapter 2 – Promises and Obligations	11
Chapter 3 – Dying and Living in the Covenant of Grace	22
Chapter 4 – Our Children in the Covenant of Grace	44
Chapter 5 – The Covenant of Grace and Public Worship	43
Appendix – Seven Essential Distinctions in the Doctrine of the Covenant of Grace	23
Recommended for Further Study	24

Preface

There once was a time when the doctrine of the covenant was a hot topic for discussion; a time, before, during and after 1944, when Reformed people were far more conversant about covenant theology than they often are today. In those days, what you believed about the covenant was a matter of the greatest importance. Believe one way and you could comfortably remain in the church of your youth. Believe another way and you could expect to be rudely shown the door. Our forefathers took their covenant theology very seriously. With the heat of those controversies so far in the past, it might be easy to forget the vital importance of understanding, believing, and living what Scripture teaches about these things. This little book is partly an effort to remind Reformed believers of this important doctrine.

It is also partly an effort to state clearly how our Reformed churches differ from much of the "New Calvinism" or "Young, Restless, and Reformed" movement. In fact, this material is a light re-working of a series of catechetical sermons delivered for the Providence Canadian Reformed Church of Hamilton in early 2014. Parishioners were asking about the differences between us and some of the "New Calvinist" churches in our area. The consistory asked me to address this in a systematic (but easily understandable) way from the pulpit.

While we may agree broadly with the "New Calvinists" about the doctrines of grace, we part ways with many of them when it comes to covenant theology. If covenant theology is essential to being Reformed (and I believe it is), it becomes rather difficult to maintain that many "New Calvinist" churches are Reformed in any meaningful way beyond the doctrines of grace. Therefore, when a Christian born and raised in a Reformed church withdraws from that church to join a "New Calvinist" group, it is an impoverishment, not an improvement.

Another purpose behind this booklet is an effort to subvert the false teaching known as Federal Vision. For some years now, Reformed and Presbyterian churches have been troubled by this movement which appears to draw from the theological heritage of the Canadian Reformed Churches, especially in regards to the doctrine of the covenant. This is not the place to outline why this movement should be regarded as deviating from confessionally Reformed orthodoxy – I have done that elsewhere.[1] Suffice it to say that I have no sympathies for this movement and, while it is not explicitly mentioned in the following pages, it was certainly in the back of my mind.

Besides those polemical purposes, I pray that readers will come away with a greater appreciation for the fact that the doctrine of the covenant of grace is a great source of gospel encouragement. In this doctrine, we find comfort, hope, and joy in Jesus Christ. In this doctrine, we discover the gracious way of life given by God and the blessed way of life before God. Whether you read this on your own for personal edification or as part of a study group in the communion of saints, my prayer for you is that the covenant of grace will be appreciated and experienced as the blessing it is intended to be.

A final note: I have tried to keep things as simple as possible in the body of the chapters. I have included a short appendix that is more geared towards the theologically inclined. There is also an annotated bibliography for those who might want to do further study in this important subject.

Wes Bredenhof
November 2014

---

1. See my *Federal Vision: A Canadian Reformed Pastor's Perspective* (Grandville: Reformed Fellowship, Inc., 2014).

CHAPTER ONE – Introducing the Big Idea

Scripture: Genesis 17:1-14; Hebrews 8:1-7
Confessions: Belgic Confession article 17

What is the covenant of grace? I once heard it explained like this: "The covenant is where God does his part and we do our part, and then we get saved and get to go to heaven." Now that explanation came from a Canadian Reformed young person and perhaps we can cut that person some slack because of their youth. However, I wonder how many of us would get it right if we were randomly asked. Would we make it sound like we believe that salvation is partly God's work and partly ours just because the covenant speaks of God's promises and our obligations?

What is the covenant of grace? That is an important question because we have attached so much importance to the covenant in our churches. It is an important part of our history. It is not an understatement to say that the Canadian Reformed Churches exist because of the doctrine of the covenant. During the 1930s and 1940s, there were intense debates about this doctrine. When the Reformed Churches in the Netherlands in the early 1940s decided to bind everyone to the views of Abraham Kuyper on the covenant (and several other doctrinal matters), that led to the Liberation of 1944. When immigrants from the Liberated Reformed Churches came over to Canada beginning in the 1950s, they were compelled to establish the Canadian Reformed Churches. So the covenant is crucially important in our history.

It is also important in the life of our churches. The covenant is behind the way we do certain things. For example, it impacts the way we view our children, the way we raise our children, and the way we educate our children. It also affects the way we worship. As we shall see later in this book, a big part of why we worship the way we do has to do again with the covenant of grace.

Covenant theology is something that really sets us apart from a lot of the other church groups around us. Even those who hold to the doctrines of grace (or TULIP)[2] usually do not hold to a Reformed doctrine of the covenant of grace. They might be Calvinistic in holding to five points about our salvation, but without the covenant, it is very difficult to view them as Reformed. A vitally important part of being Reformed is being covenantal.

If it is true that it is so crucially important, someone might raise a question: why is the covenant of grace not mentioned more often in our confessions? It is true that the covenant is mentioned only a few times in the Three Forms of Unity. For example, in the Heidelberg Catechism, it's only mentioned in the Lord's Days dealing with the sacraments. Lord's Day 27 mentions the covenant in connection with infant baptism and Lord's Day 30 mentions it in connection with the Lord's Supper. But other than that, the covenant is not explicitly mentioned in the Heidelberg Catechism anywhere else. Why is that? Probably at least partly because the Catechism was originally meant to be a teaching tool for children and young people. In Heidelberg in the sixteenth century, the doctrine of the covenant was considered to be more meat than milk. Zacharias Ursinus wrote another catechism for use with his seminary students.[3] That catechism mentions the covenant in many places and works out the doctrine in more detail, providing the meat seminary students need.

Certainly we can say that this doctrine has always been important in Reformed churches, even if it is not especially prominent in our

---

2. These are the five points found in the Canons of Dort: Total Depravity, Unconditional Election, Limited Atonement, Irresistible Grace, and Perseverance of the Saints. While each of them can be described better, these are the terms commonly used and abbreviated with the memorable acronym TULIP.

3. Ursinus' Larger Catechism can be found in Lyle D. Bierma, *An Introduction to the Heidelberg Catechism: Sources, History, Theology* (Grand Rapids: Baker Academic, 2005), 163-223. It can also be found online here: http://links.christreformed.org/doctrinevision/ursinus_project.pdf

confessions. Because it is so important, it is good that we give some dedicated attention to it. Over the following chapters, we are going to look at the basic shape of the doctrine of the covenant of grace and why it is so important for us as Reformed believers.

Now it would be very easy to make this rather complicated. It **is** a meaty doctrine and the potential is there to go over the heads of nearly every reader. That is the last thing I want. I want everyone reading this to have a solid basic understanding of the covenant of grace. I am going to do my best to keep it as simple and straightforward as I can. Some readers will already have read or studied more on this subject and may be wondering why this or that is not being discussed. It is not necessarily because it is unimportant; it is just that I do not want to lose anybody as we go through this. I am not writing for theologians, but for regular church members.

In that line, let me narrow our focus here. We are going to focus on the covenant of grace as we encounter it in our lives as believers in this day and age. We are not going to get into questions about whether there is a covenant between the three persons of the Trinity regarding our salvation. We are not going to get into questions about whether the relationship between God and Adam before the fall into sin was a covenant relationship and if so, how we should speak about it. I am not going to discuss Hittite vassal treaties or the development of different covenant administrations through the course of redemptive history. These are all interesting questions and they are certainly important, but we want to keep everything as simple as possible. So, in this book, our focus will be on the covenant of grace in our lives today.

I have one last introductory comment. This is a gospel doctrine. After all, it is a covenant **of grace**. This doctrine speaks to us powerfully about the grace of God, which is good news for sinners. I really want to bring that out in the following pages. Too often, the covenant of grace has been misunderstood as a burdensome or legalistic thing. We deny works in our salvation with the Five Points (TULIP) and so on, but then inadvertently reintroduce them with our covenant doctrine. Remember the young person who thought that the covenant was God doing his part, and us doing our part? That is not the gospel. That is not a covenant **of grace**. As we are going to see, in the Bible, the covenant of grace is a gospel blessing. It is something to treasure and embrace with both our minds and our hearts.

The Essence of the Covenant of Grace

So we turn again to that question: what is the covenant of grace? How do we define it? The Bible leads us to think of it along the lines of marriage. When you attend a wedding, you watch bride and groom exchange vows with another. They make promises and commitments to one another. These vows establish the marriage. Soon after the vows, the couple go over to a table and sign some legal forms. These forms also play a role in establishing the marriage. The vows and the legal forms are important, but no one would seriously argue that the marriage consists of those things. Those things are foundational and necessary, but they do not make up the essence of the marriage. What is the essence of a marriage? It is a relationship. While marriage is established by vows, promises, commitments and other things, the essence is a relationship. It is the same thing with the covenant. The covenant of grace is essentially a relationship between God and his people.

That comparison comes out in Scripture in several places. One of those places is in the prophecy of Hosea. Hosea married an unfaithful woman and then the LORD used that broken marriage to illustrate the broken covenant relationship with his people. He explicitly and directly compares his covenant with Israel to a marriage relationship. The amazing thing is that even though that relationship is broken, God does not stop loving his spouse. He takes the initiative, goes after her and will redeem her and repair the relationship. We can see this in Hosea 2:14-23:

> 14 "Therefore, behold, I will allure her,
>   and bring her into the wilderness,
>   and speak tenderly to her.
> 15 And there I will give her her vineyards

and make the Valley of Achor a door of hope.
And there she shall answer as in the days of her youth,
as at the time when she came out of the land of Egypt.

[16] "And in that day, declares the Lord, you will call me 'My Husband,' and no longer will you call me 'My Baal.'
[17] For I will remove the names of the Baals from her mouth, and they shall be remembered by name no more.
[18] And I will make for them a covenant on that day with the beasts of the field, the birds of the heavens, and the creeping things of the ground. And I will abolish the bow, the sword, and war from the land, and I will make you lie down in safety.
[19] And I will betroth you to me forever.
I will betroth you to me in righteousness and in justice, in steadfast love and in mercy.
[20] I will betroth you to me in faithfulness. And you shall know the Lord.

[21] "And in that day I will answer, declares the Lord,
I will answer the heavens, and they shall answer the earth,
[22] and the earth shall answer the grain, the wine,
and the oil, and they shall answer Jezreel,
[23] and I will sow her for myself in the land.
And I will have mercy on No Mercy,
and I will say to Not My People,
'You are my people'; and he shall say, 'You are my God.'"

That's grace functioning in this covenant relationship!

Notice how that passage ended, "you are my people," "you are my God." That kind of language is also found in Genesis 17 when God establishes his covenant with Abraham. The LORD says clearly that he will be their God. They will be his people and that will be shown through circumcision. The LORD being their God and they being his people again speaks of a relationship. There is a close bond and connection between them.

Now you might be thinking, "I thought we were going to be looking at the covenant of grace as we experience it as believers today. But we're in the Old Testament here, looking at Hosea and now Abraham. That's not today!" But hold on one moment. You need to look carefully at Genesis 17, especially verse 7:

> And I will establish my covenant between me and you and your offspring after you throughout their generations for an everlasting covenant, to be God to you and to your offspring after you.

God speaks there of an "everlasting covenant" with Abraham and his people. This covenant relationship is going to be in effect forever, from that point forward. It is still in effect today – it includes us.

This is confirmed by what we read in the New Testament, especially in Galatians 3. In that chapter, Paul connects Christians today to Abraham in Genesis. In verse 7, he says, "Know then that it is those of faith who are the sons of Abraham." And in verse 29, "And if you are Christ's, then you are Abraham's offspring, heirs according to the promise." In other words, you are in that everlasting covenant relationship between God and his people that included Abraham thousands of years ago. In that sense, your experience of the covenant of grace is similar to what Abraham experienced. He and his people had a relationship with God and so do you.

The Origins of the Covenant of Grace

Now what about the origins of the covenant of grace? As I said in the introduction, I am not going to trace the historical development of the covenant and its varied administrations in Scripture. What we are interested in is the question of **who** originated the covenant of grace that we enjoy today. So when we talk about origins, we are going at the question of **who** is really behind it. **Whose** big idea is this?

Article 17 of the Belgic Confession does not mention the word "covenant," but what it says is definitely covenantal:

We believe that, when He saw that man had thus plunged himself into physical and spiritual death and made himself completely miserable, our gracious God in His marvellous wisdom and goodness set out to seek man when he trembling fled from Him. He comforted him with the promise that He would give him His Son, born of woman (Gal 4:4), to crush the head of the serpent and to make man blessed.

That article speaks of the fall into sin, summarizing what Scripture says in Genesis 3. After Adam and Eve plunged themselves into a world of hurt, God did not abandon them. He sought to restore his relationship with them -- a **covenant relationship**. The key thing to note there is that it was God who took the initiative. Just as God took the initiative to create man, so also God took the initiative to redeem man and restore his relationship with him.

Therefore we insist that the origins of the covenant of grace are with God. God is the one who began this relationship of grace with his people. God sought Adam and Eve. Further down in history, God went after Abraham. In Joshua 24, we read of the covenant renewal ceremony at Shechem. Joshua speaks the Word of the LORD to the people. God says in verses 2 and 3 of Joshua 24, "Long ago, your fathers lived beyond the Euphrates, Terah the father of Abraham and of Nahor; and they served other gods. Then I took your father Abraham from beyond the River and led him through all the land of Canaan, and made his offspring many." Abraham and his forefathers were idol worshippers, not seeking after God. But it was God who came after Abraham. This is why it says, "**I** took your father Abraham from beyond the river." The LORD graciously took the initiative, not Abraham.

These things are true for us today too. No matter how we came into this covenant relationship with God, we cannot ever claim any credit for it ourselves. God has taken the initiative to pursue us and bring us into this people who have a special bond with him.

The origins are a vital part of why it is called the covenant **of grace**. God did not owe it to Adam to come after him in the garden. God was under no obligation, especially after Adam had slapped him in the face by listening to the serpent. Abraham was no better, worshipping idols with his fathers in Ur of the Chaldeans. God was not compelled in any way to set his love upon Abraham and call him out of idolatry. Abraham did not deserve it. Neither do any of us deserve a covenant relationship with the LORD. Of ourselves, we do not have a right to it and he does not owe it to us. This is one of the important reasons why it is called the covenant **of grace**. In his mercy and kindness, he gives us the relationship that we do not deserve. He sets his love on us and says, "I am your God and you are my people. We have an everlasting bond." That is grace and we should not stop being amazed at it. You should never take it for granted that you have been blessed in this way. Be thankful and praise God that he has included you in his covenant people!

The Parties in the Covenant of Grace

I have already mentioned who are the parties in this covenant of grace. There are no surprises here. On the one side there is God. He initiates and establishes the covenant of grace. Then there is us, the people of God.

However, we can and must develop this further. If we look at Genesis 17 again, the relationship described there is not only between God and believing Abraham, but also with his offspring, his children. That everlasting covenant is a relationship between God and believers, together with the children of believers. It is extremely important to recognize that the children of believers are also included in the covenant of grace.

Now someone might say, "Well, that was in the Old Testament for the Jews. For Christians today, it's different. It's a new covenant and that new covenant is only between God and believers, it doesn't include the children of believers." In response, I would draw your attention to Ephesians 6. In that chapter, Paul addresses the children of the Ephesian church. It is quite remarkable how he addresses them. He says in Ephesians 6:1, "Children, obey your parents in the Lord, for this is right." And then in the following verse he appeals to the Fifth Commandment and its promise, "that it may go well with you and that you may live long in the land." The Ten Words of the Covenant are applied to the children of the Ephesian church. Have you ever noticed that before? Why does Paul write like this? Because those children in the Ephesian church are included in the covenant of grace. Paul can appeal to them as covenant people with the covenant law and covenant promises, because they are covenant children.

Therefore, we maintain that the covenant of grace is with believers **and** their children. The parties in the covenant of grace are God together with believers and their offspring. Yet there is someone else involved in the covenant and we cannot forget about him. His involvement in this covenant of grace is crucially important for it to function in a good way. There is a Mediator in the covenant of grace.

By nature, we as human beings are at war with God. In ourselves, without the Holy Spirit, we hate God and we wage war against him. That makes it impossible for a holy God to be in a friendly relationship with us. We need a Mediator, someone to bring the parties together in the relationship.

That is what Jesus Christ does for us. According to Hebrews 8, he is the Mediator of the covenant administration which we experience and live under today. Christ came with the sacrifice that could atone for our sins. He offers the sacrifice that could turn away the wrath of God. He makes propitiation for us (propitiation means that wrath is turned away and favour is restored). With Christ's redemptive work, we are reconciled to God. That word "reconciled," speaks of a friendly relationship. That friendly relationship is a covenant relationship.

So also when we look at the Mediator of the covenant, we come to understand that this is indeed a covenant **of grace**. This speaks to us of the gospel. We have a Saviour who makes a healthy relationship between a holy God and a sinful people work. It does not depend on us, but on him. Without Christ the Mediator, there would be no covenant of grace. There would be no relationship of peace with our Creator.

With that in mind, I want to urge you to continue looking to our Mediator in faith. Without him, this relationship would not be established. Without him, this relationship would have no hope of continuing in a healthy way. You need Jesus Christ in the covenant of grace. The covenant of grace does not replace Jesus Christ, as if you could have the covenant instead of him. Rather, the covenant depends on Christ and here too we desperately need him. We must not look to ourselves in any way, but only to our Saviour, because everything hangs on him.

As we conclude this chapter, let us review what we have learned. The essence of the covenant is a relationship. The origins of the covenant are with God – hence we speak of the covenant of grace. The parties in the covenant are God, believers and their children, with Christ as the Mediator. With the big idea now sketched out, we can proceed to look at the covenant of grace in more detail.

Questions for Reflection and Discussion

1. Why is there a persistent temptation to make the covenant of grace into another form of works-salvation?

2. What is the role of the Holy Spirit in the covenant of grace?

3. What are some potential dangers associated with speaking of the covenant of grace as a legal agreement or contract?

4. As noted above, the parties in the covenant of grace are God together with believers and their children, with Christ as Mediator. Does the covenant of grace have any significance for the created world around us?

5. How would you evaluate the following statement? "In our churches, we need to speak less about the covenant and more about the gospel."

CHAPTER TWO – **Promises and Obligations**

Scripture: 2 Corinthians 6:1-7:1
Confessions: Heidelberg Catechism QA 94

In this chapter we want to look at the terms by which the covenant relationship functions. What is the framework of this relationship as it gets lived out between God and his people? This is where we encounter those familiar words: promise and obligation. Where do those words come from? It might surprise you, but we do not find those words in our confessions anywhere. They are not in the Heidelberg Catechism or Belgic Confession or Canons of Dort. One might argue that the idea is there in some form, but the exact words are not. The exact words come from our Forms for Baptism (Infant and Adult). Our Forms for Baptism both give a time-tested and well-formulated overview of biblical teaching on the sacrament. We read that "every covenant contains two parts, a promise and an obligation." This is precisely right and this is what we are going to look at in this chapter. What does God promise in the covenant of grace? What is expected of us in the covenant of grace?

The Promises of the Covenant of Grace

We begin with God and what he graciously promises us. In the last chapter, I said that we want to keep things as simple as we can when it comes to this doctrine. When it comes to the divine promises in the covenant of grace, we can summarize them with one sentence: "I will be your God and you will be my people." Those words are found throughout Scripture in relation to the covenant relationship.[4] Those words are also found in 2 Corinthians 6:

---

4. For example: Exodus 6:7, Jeremiah 7:23, Jeremiah 11:4, Jeremiah 30:22, and Ezekiel 36:28.

[16] What agreement has the temple of God with idols?
For we are the temple of the living God; as God said,

"I will make my dwelling among them and walk
among them, and I will be their God,
and they shall be my people.
[17] Therefore go out from their midst,
and be separate from them, says the Lord,
and touch no unclean thing;
then I will welcome you,
[18] and I will be a father to you,
and you shall be sons and daughters to me, says the Lord
Almighty."

Paul quotes from Leviticus 26:12, "I will be their God and they shall be my people." Right there you basically have what God promises in the covenant. He promises to be our God and he promises that we will be his people. He promises himself to us, he promises that he will be ours and we will be his. He promises an eternal bond or connection between himself and us, a bond of fellowship and love.

But we can go further than this basic summary. In fact, why would you not want to? Surely you want to hear more of what God promises us in the covenant. After all, this is entirely gospel grace. It is all beautiful and encouraging for believers. So let me unpack what it means that God promises to be our God and what it means that God promises that we will be his people.

We can do that with the help of the Heidelberg Catechism. As I mentioned, the exact words "promise and obligation" are never used in the Catechism. Yet promise by itself is definitely there! In Lord's Day 7, we hear about true faith in QA 21. Then QA 22 goes on to ask, "What, then, must a Christian believe?" The answer: "All that is promised us in the gospel, which the articles of our catholic and undoubted Christian faith teach us in a summary."

While that is a good answer, you might be thinking to yourself, "What does that have to do with the covenant of grace? One minute you're speaking about the promises of the covenant and then the next about all that is promised us in the gospel. Isn't that a leap?" No, that is not a leap at all. The promises of the covenant of grace **are** the gospel promises. What God promises us in the covenant of grace is everything bound up with the good news.

Certainly that is the way things were viewed by Zacharias Ursinus, the main author of our Catechism. As mentioned in the last chapter, the Heidelberg Catechism was first written for children. It was written to instruct the youth of that German-speaking region known as the Palatinate. However, Ursinus also wrote two other catechisms. His Large Catechism was used for the training of seminary students. It follows the basic structure of the Heidelberg Catechism. It also works out some of the teachings of the Heidelberg Catechism in more detail. QA 35 of Ursinus' Large Catechism reads,

Question: What does the gospel teach?

Answer: It teaches what God promises us in the covenant of his grace, how we are received into it, and how we know we are in it; that is, how we are set free from sin and death and how we are certain of this deliverance.[5]

Do you see it? The promises of the gospel are the promises of the covenant of grace. The gospel is covenantal.

So what does God promise us in the gospel? Let us review with the help of the biblical summary found in Lord's Days 9-22 of the Heidelberg Catechism.[6] Let us be reminded of how beautiful and precious all these promises are.

---

5. Bierma, *An Introduction to the Heidelberg Catechism*, 168.
6. For the biblical support for each of these promises, refer to the Lord's Day mentioned.

He promises that for the sake of Christ, he will be our God and Father. He promises to provide us with everything we need for body and soul. He says that he will turn to our good whatever adversity

he sends in this life of sorrow (Lord's Day 9). God promises us that no creature shall separate us from his love (Lord's Day 10).

He also promises that through Jesus he will save us from all our sins (Lord's Day 11). He will make sure that the penalty is paid for our sins, and perfect obedience is offered in our place. He promises us that in Christ we have a prophet who will teach us all we need to know about our redemption. He promises that in Christ we have a priest who will redeem us with his sacrifice and intercede for us forever before him in heaven. He promises us an eternal King in Christ who will rule us with his Word and Spirit and defend and preserve us in our salvation (Lord's Day 12). These are truly wonderful promises! They are full of grace and designed to give us comfort and joy.

The promises go on. He promises that we are his beloved adopted children through his grace in Christ (Lord's Day 13, QA 33). We are promised that we have been ransomed with the precious blood of Jesus so that we can be his own possession (Lord's Day 13, QA 34). He promises that this is a good place to be. God promises that our original sin is covered with the innocence of our Mediator (Lord's Day 14). Moreover, he promises that by the suffering of Christ, our body and soul have been redeemed from everlasting wrath. He promises us incredible gifts: the grace of God, righteousness, and eternal life. We are promised freedom from the severe judgment of God that we deserved; the curse which lay on us has been taken by another, by Jesus (Lord's Day 15).

The covenantal gospel promises that when we die, our death is not a payment for sin, but gives us entrance into the life that lasts forever. Death has died in the death of Christ. God promises that our old nature too has been dealt a death blow. He promises to give us a new identity, a new nature whereby we can offer up living sacrifices of gratitude to him (Lord's Day 16).

How about more promises? The covenantal gospel promises us that death has been overcome by Christ in his death and resurrection. God promises us a resurrection hope, a new life now already, and later our own glorious resurrection (Lord's Day 17). He promises us that at this very moment we have a voice in heaven on our behalf. We have someone speaking for us, one who is our Advocate. Some day he promises to take us to himself in glory. But, for now, he promises us his Spirit who gives us power to seek the things that are above (Lord's Day 18). Additionally, he promises us that someday he will come again to deliver us and all his people (Lord's Day 19).

There are also promises connected with the Holy Spirit. God promises to give his Holy Spirit so that we can share in Christ and all his benefits, so that we can be comforted (Lord's Day 20). He promises us a place in his holy Church and in the communion of saints. The gospel promises us that we can have communion with Christ and share in all his treasures and gifts (Lord's Day 21, QAs 54 and 55).

Then, of course, there is the forgiveness of sins. God promises us forgiveness through Christ of all our sins, past, present and future. He promises to take them out of the way, to forget them, to throw them in the depths of the sea, to remove them as far as the east is from the west. This is all because of our Saviour Jesus (Lord's Day 21, QA 56). Also through him, we are promised the resurrection of the body. On his great day, he promises that our bodies will be raised in glory to live forever in the new heavens and new earth. (Lord's Day 22, QA 57) The gospel promises us perfect blessedness in the life everlasting. A perfect blessedness is held out to us that no one has yet seen or heard of and in that blessed state all of God's people will praise him forever (Lord's Day 22, QA 58). There are so many riches bound up with the covenantal gospel promises! Is it not amazing what God holds out to us in his grace?

Now I want to emphasize as clearly as I can that all of that is promised **to every single person** in the covenant of grace. There are **no** exceptions. These promises come to all believers and their children, head for head. The covenantal gospel promises are widely distributed to one and all in this relationship.

Someone might hear that and conclude, "Then everyone in the covenant must be saved. If God proclaims his gospel promises to one and all, then all in the covenant must be saved. You must be saying that salvation is automatic." Unfortunately, this is the way that the doctrine of the covenant has sometimes been seriously misunderstood. Some have used that misunderstanding to justify living in sin. They think to themselves, "I can live however I want, because I'm a covenant child. God has given me these promises and God is God, so I'm saved no matter what I do. I can live like the devil and it really doesn't matter because I'm in the covenant and I have the promises." This is a most wicked and sinful way of thinking. It is a complete perversion of the biblical doctrine of the covenant of grace. Those who think that way are on the broad road that leads to destruction.

You must read carefully here. It would be easy to misunderstand what you are about to read. We must distinguish between **extending** the promise and **receiving** what is promised.

An illustration might help. It is not a perfect illustration, but it will get the point across. Imagine if I were to give you a cheque for $10,000. Another name for a cheque is a promissory note. It is a promise from me that you will receive $10,000 from my bank account. But say that you take my cheque and put it in your pocket and then forget about it. Next week you pull those pants on and you put your hand in your pocket and there is a crumpled wad of paper. It has been through the washing machine, and you are not quite sure what it is anymore. You throw it in the garbage.

Did I extend a promise of $10,000? **Yes**, I wrote the cheque and gave that promissory note to you.

However, did you receive $10,000? **No**, because you did not take the cheque to the bank and deposit it or cash it. You did not do anything with that cheque and so you missed out on what was promised.

Do you see the difference now? It is the difference between extending a promise and receiving what has been promised. It is the difference between giving a cheque for $10,000 and getting $10,000 in your hand.

That is what happens in the covenant of grace. God proclaims the promises of the covenant to all in the covenant. **Every single person** -- and that needs to be stressed. However, not every single person receives **what** is promised in the covenant: the blessings. That is because there is a human responsibility within the covenant relationship. Everybody needs to bring the cheque to the bank, so to speak. The big question is: How do we do that? That brings us to the covenant obligations.

The Obligations of the Covenant of Grace

We are in a dangerous spot here. To get to Vancouver Island, most people take a ferry from Vancouver. If you go from Tsawwassen to Swartz Bay, the ferry goes through this rather narrow passage of water called Active Pass. It is an L-shaped passage, a dog-leg with Mayne Island on one side and Galiano Island on the other. To get a large ferry through Active Pass is not easy – the people at the helm have to be paying careful attention. It would be easy to get ship-wrecked on one side or the other. Something similar can happen when we are discussing obligations in the covenant.

On one side, there is this view that there are no obligations in the covenant. You are in and you are automatically saved and you can believe and live however you want. We could call this the Godless Rocks. You could get ship-wrecked on this wrong view of covenant obligations; you could get ship-wrecked on the Godless Rocks.

On the other side, there is this other view that your covenant obedience to God's law merits salvation. God does his part, you do your part, and the result is salvation. You get in the covenant by God's grace, but you stay in by your works of faithful obedience.

This is a legalistic view of covenant obligations. We could call this the Legalistic Rocks. You could get ship-wrecked on the Legalistic Rocks too. While insisting that you hold to the doctrines of grace as outlined in the Canons of Dort, you could be blindly living by a sort of practical Arminianism through your doctrine of the covenant. Your view of covenant obligations could make you essentially into an Arminian, a walking contradiction. Salvation is all by grace, but it still depends on you.

So, on the one side there are the Godless Rocks. On the other are the Legalistic Rocks. Both are dangerous and destructive. We need to safely and carefully steer a course between these. How do we do that?

We do that by keeping first things first. What the Bible puts first is what we put first. In terms of human responsibility before God, the first thing God calls for is **faith**. He calls us to take him at his Word and believe his promises. Do you remember how I wrote that the promises of the covenant could be boiled down to what God says in 2 Corinthians 6:16, "I will be their God and they shall be my people"? Well, the obligation of the covenant can also be boiled down to that. It can be boiled down to our responding with, "He shall be our God and we will be his people." That is the response of faith.

Just as with the promises, however, we can and should go deeper. God calls us to believe in him, to trust his Word, especially to take all his gospel promises and make them our own. This is really what the first commandment comes down to. We sometimes call the Ten Commandments "God's covenant law." As you know, God's covenant law begins with "I am the LORD your God who brought you out of Egypt, out of the land of slavery." It begins with a word of grace and deliverance. Then it immediately follows with the first commandment, "You shall have no other gods before me." That is another way of saying, "He shall be our God and we will be his people." We will not entrust ourselves to anyone else; we shall not look to anyone else in faith. We will depend on no one else but God only.

The explanation of the first commandment in Question and Answer 94 of the Catechism is excellent on this:

Q. What does the Lord require in the first commandment?

A. That for the sake of my very salvation I avoid and flee all idolatry, witchcraft, superstition, and prayer to saints or to other creatures. Further, that I rightly come to know the only true God, trust in Him alone, submit to Him with all humility and patience, expect all good from Him only, and love, fear, and honour Him with all my heart. In short, that I forsake all creatures rather than do the least thing against His will.

Not only are we to steer away from anything that might replace God, but we are to rightly know him and **trust** in him alone. We are to love, fear, and honour him, submit to him, and expect all good only from him. All these are different ways of speaking about faith; they are faith considered from different angles. What does the first commandment really call us to? It calls us to faith in the true God; to believe him and have him only as our God. That is our all-important starting point when it comes to the obligations of the covenant. Take God at his Word and trust him. Specifically, believe all that he has promised you in the gospel. Believe that in Jesus Christ, he is your Father to whom you are inseparably bound. When he says, "I am your God and you belong to me," our reply is, "Yes, LORD, you are my God and I do belong to you through Jesus. I believe what you say about yourself and about me. I am yours, save me." You see, faith is the way we take the cheque to the bank, so to speak. We receive all that is promised us in the gospel when we believe that these things are true for us individually and personally. God calls us to faith and by that we can see that there is nothing automatic in the covenant of grace. You do not receive all that is promised in an automatic way – you need to believe God for yourself and take those promises and apply them to yourself in faith.

When we have true faith, there will always be fruit. When you are truly united to Christ through faith, you are grafted into the vine, and you will bear fruit (John 15:5). Within the covenant relationship, God wants us to believe in him and take him at his Word, and so expects to see this fruit from those who believe in him. That means that he wants his children in Christ to embrace not only what he has promised in the gospel for our deliverance, but also what he commands in the law for our growth in holiness. Moreover, within the covenant of grace, those with true faith actually more and more **desire** to do this. Therefore, this obedience to God's law is not a legalistic obligation imposed on us, but something that wells up from hearts that have been touched by the grace of God. It comes from hearts that are being shaped by his grace. As we read and hear God's Word, we increasingly **want** to live in holiness before God already in this life. True faith bears the kind of fruit that God expects. It bears the fruit of holy and godly living.

In 2 Corinthians 6, that was worked out in regard to a particular pastoral issue. The issue was marriage between believers and unbelievers. Of course, that is an issue that is still around today. Paul says that the LORD is your God and you are his people. There is a bond between you and him. Believe that and then let that bear fruit in your life, also when it comes to whom you marry. Because the LORD is your God and you are his people, you will not be yoked with (hitched up to) an unbeliever – you cannot. You will not get into romantic relationships with unbelievers, because you know that this does not follow from your faith in what your covenant God has said about you and him. Here the covenant does not lead to "I can do whatever I want and it doesn't matter because salvation is automatic." Instead, the covenant relationship leads to "I want to follow the LORD because he has graciously entered into fellowship with me and given me rich promises in Christ and I believe him." It leads to what Psalm 119:97 says, "Oh how I love your law! It is my meditation all the day."

As we reflect further on this with an open Bible, we realize that this too is God's work of grace in our lives. He not only gives the covenant obligations, he also enables us to meet them. After all, faith is a gift of the Holy Spirit according to Paul in Ephesians 2:8. The fruit of our faith – holy living – is also Christ's work in us through his Word and Spirit. While we insist on the reality of human responsibility within the covenant of grace, we also recognize that God's grace is behind everything good that happens in this relationship. This is why we call it the covenant **of grace**. So in the covenant, it is never a matter of "we get in by grace, and we stay in by works." Why? Because on the one hand, once God has placed you in that covenant relationship, you are always in that relationship. It does not mean that this relationship always works to your blessing, but it is always a reality. On the other hand, when it does work to your blessing, it is entirely by grace. God's grace determines everything good. He gives you the Mediator of the covenant and he gives the means by which you take hold of that Mediator – he gives the gift of faith. Therefore, you can never take any credit for yourself. All the glory belongs to God within the covenant relationship.

Yet there might be a lingering question in someone's mind. What if there is no fruit? Someone says, "What if I look at my life and there's no desire for holiness? I don't want to grow as a Christian and I have no interest in the Bible or spiritual things. I don't like being told about my sin and I don't want to change. To tell you the truth, I don't really like going to church. But I still believe in God." Can such a person receive what is promised in the covenant of grace?

To answer that, we should first go to the words of Christ in John 15:4-5.

> [4] Abide in me, and I in you. As the branch cannot bear fruit by itself, unless it abides in the vine, neither can you, unless you abide in me. [5] I am the vine; you are the branches. Whoever abides in me and I in him, he it is that bears much fruit, for apart from me you can do nothing.

When you are in Christ by faith, you bear fruit. If you are apart from Christ, you do nothing fruitful before God. If there is no fruit, then you are not in Christ. That is the logical conclusion of what we read here. Christ was speaking to his disciples who claimed to believe in him. He insists that the evidence of faith is in its fruit. Everyone who has a true faith will bear some fruit, and the design is to bear increasingly greater fruit. However, if there is no fruit, then there cannot be any faith either. If there is no faith, that person cannot receive what is promised in the covenant of grace. That does not mean that they are cast out of the covenant. Rather, it just means that they are not receiving what is promised and the covenant relationship is not blessing them. There are consequences attached to being in the covenant and being unbelieving, but we will learn about that in the next chapter.

For now, notice what Paul says in 2 Corinthians 7:1. He says, "Since we have these promises, beloved, let us cleanse ourselves from every defilement of body and spirit, bringing holiness to completion in the fear of God." Notice how the application follows from the promises. We hear those promises, we believe them, and then we want to live accordingly. We want to be living in holiness according to the Word of God. When that desire is not there, then we need to hear the warning of Hebrews 12:14, "Strive for peace with everyone, **and for the holiness without which no one will see the Lord**." You will never see the Lord without holiness, that is abundantly clear. Where does personal holiness begin? It begins with faith, with believing in the Lord's promises. Personal holiness is always a fruit of true faith. Personal holiness, even in the smallest measures, never exists apart from true faith in Christ. If there is no fruit, there is no faith. And if there is no faith, there are no covenant blessings.

Each reader needs to personally take hold of what God promises in the gospel. That is first and foremost. Let me say it one more time in case anyone missed it: there is nothing automatic in the covenant. You are not going to be saved just because you were born in the covenant to believing parents. If you are going to live in sin, you are going to hell whether or not you are a covenant child. You will be saved when you repent of your sins and turn to Jesus Christ in faith, believing in the Mediator of the covenant, and resting and trusting in him alone. God has said, "I am your God, you are my people." Believe him. Walk with him.

Questions for Reflection and Discussion

1. Prove from Scripture the statement that every church member (youngest to oldest, believer and unbeliever/hypocrite, elect and reprobate) is included in the covenant of grace and therefore a recipient of all the promises.

2. Which is a more dangerous threat today, the Godless Rocks or the Legalistic Rocks? Why? How should we address the one you identified as most dangerous?

3. We saw that faith is the first and foremost obligation of the covenant. How would you evaluate an approach which agrees that faith is primary, but then includes obedience to the law in the definition of faith?

4. What is the connection between the means of grace (preaching and sacraments) and the promises and obligations of the covenant of grace? Why is this connection so important and what bearing should that have on your life?

5. It has been said that "the covenant of grace is one-sided in its origin and two-sided in its existence." Is this an accurate statement? Why or why not?

CHAPTER THREE – **Dying and Living in the Covenant of Grace**

**Scripture: Hebrews 12
Confessions: Heidelberg Catechism Lord's Day 31**

Let me briefly review what we have learned thus far. In the first chapter, we saw that the essence of the covenant is a relationship. Believers **and** their children are in a covenant relationship with God. Christ is the Mediator of this relationship. It is only through his intercession that this relationship functions in a healthy way. It is only through Jesus that a sinful people can be in a peaceful relationship with a holy God and be under his blessings.

Last chapter we went further and learned about the promises and obligations in the covenant of grace. Both the promises and the obligations can be summed up with that expression found throughout Scripture, "I will be your God and you will be my people." That can be teased out further. The covenant promises are everything that is promised to us in the gospel. The first and foremost covenant obligation is faith, to trust God and his promises in Jesus Christ. There is nothing automatic in the covenant. God's people are called to believe him and take him at his Word. I used the illustration of a cheque. If you do not cash the cheque, you do not receive what the cheque promises. Similarly, in the covenant of grace, you need to cash the cheque, so to speak. The way you do that, the way you receive what is promised, is through faith. Moreover, as we saw, true faith will and must always bear fruit in holy living. This is what God expects to see from his covenant people. He wants to see people who believe what he has promised and then bear the fruit of godliness. Now in this chapter we are going to take what we have learned so far and build further on it.

The key thing to understand in this chapter is that there are two ways of relating to God in the covenant of grace. The first is the way of faith, the way to life and blessing. The other is the way of unbelief. This is the way to death and curse. God holds out both these ways before us in his Word. One is held out to us to attract and entice us -- to woo us, if you will. The other is held out to warn us, even to threaten us.

The Way to Death and Curse

It might not seem very pleasant to read about death and curse. Yet perhaps there may be some readers who need to hear this message. Perhaps some who are reading are presently living unrepentantly in unbelief and this is the day that God is going to wake them up. Maybe this is the moment when someone living in the way of death finally hears the voice of God calling him or her to the better way, the way of life and blessing. It would be a cruel kindness to be silent about these important things.

Lord's Day 31 clearly outlines the two ways of relating to God in the covenant, particularly in QA 84:

Q. How is the kingdom of heaven opened and closed by the preaching of the gospel?

A. According to the command of Christ, the kingdom of heaven is opened when it is proclaimed and publicly testified to each and every believer that God has really forgiven all their sins for the sake of Christ's merits, as often as they by true faith accept the promise of the gospel. The kingdom of heaven is closed when it is proclaimed and testified to all unbelievers and hypocrites that the wrath of God and eternal condemnation rest on them as long as they do not repent. According to this testimony of the gospel, God will judge both in this life and in the life to come.

The two ways of relating to God are found in what we confess there. When the gospel is preached, people react. There is always a response to the preaching of God's Word. Sometimes the response is good; people take it in like they are hearing it for the first time. Sometimes the response is bad; some do not even make the effort to look like they are listening, while others look like they are listening but in their minds they are off somewhere else. Sometimes it varies. Yet there is **always** some kind of response. No one walks away from the preaching of the gospel without some response one way or another.

Sadly, there are those who hear the preaching of the gospel, but they do not believe and do not repent. According to our confession, it should be proclaimed and testified to unbelievers and hypocrites in the church that they are under the wrath of God. They have eternal condemnation resting upon them. God will be their judge. Preachers are called to give the solemn warning of God's Word: if you are going to be saved from the coming wrath, you need to turn away from your sin and turn to Jesus in faith. You need to believe in him and him only. If you do not, if you remain in sin, you are going to hell. Without true faith in Christ, you are facing an eternal conscious torment under God's wrath.

Being a covenant child does dramatically change things here, but not for the better. If you were born to believing parents, you are in the covenant of grace. God has promised many wonderful things to you. However, there is the reality that some in the covenant slap God in the face, they spurn him. They turn away from his promises and his claims on them. They say, "At my baptism, you publically said I belong to you. But I say I belong to me. I'm going to live life my way, not yours. I'm not going to believe your promises; I'm going to follow my own path. God, I really want nothing to do with you." In some instances, the person saying this leaves everything behind. They leave the church and plunge headlong into a life of sin. They strive for some kind of consistency in their unbelief. After all, why go to church on Sunday and waste your time listening to a message you do not even believe? Yet others hang on. For whatever reason, they continue going to church, even if only irregularly. They continue to be members of the church, at least on paper. Perhaps they do it to please their parents or grandparents. However, the reality is that their heart is stone-cold to God. In private or with non-Christian friends, this person lives in sin and acts like the unbeliever that he or she really is. They may have covered it up well enough that they can remain a member in good standing in the church. Yet God knows the heart (Luke 16:15). He sees and he knows. Moreover, he will judge. As Jesus pointedly says in Luke 12:48, "Everyone to whom much is given, of him much will be required".

That means God will judge the covenant child who lives in unbelief **far more harshly** than the average vanilla unbeliever. This teaching is also clear throughout the book of Hebrews. In 12:24, the author of Hebrews warns his readers to not refuse God who is speaking to them "a better word than the blood of Abel." The God who is a consuming fire is warning us from heaven, calling for faith. If we refuse him, there will be serious consequences. Earlier in Hebrews, this gets worked out in more detail. In Hebrews 6, the author says that if you fall away and refuse to believe, you are crucifying again the Son of God and holding him up to contempt. You are spitting in the face of Jesus – a horrible thing to do. We are warned that this is the way of covenant curse.

This is what the Jews did to Jesus. These covenant people heard his preaching and then the preaching of the apostles. Some believed, but many refused the call of the gospel. In Matthew 11, Christ addressed this unbelief among the covenant people. There were towns of covenant people like you and me -- towns like Chorazin, Bethsaida, and Capernaum. They did not repent. They refused to turn from their sin and believe in Jesus. This is where we find those earth-shattering words of Jesus in Matthew 11:23-24:

> And you, Capernaum, will you be exalted to heaven? You will be brought down to Hades. For if the mighty works done in you had been done in Sodom, it would have remained until this day. But I tell you that it will be more tolerable on the day of judgment for the land of Sodom than for you.

Those are weighty words and you need to feel their weight. We need to hear those words in the light of Jude 7, "…just as Sodom and Gomorrah and the surrounding cities, which likewise indulged in sexual immorality and pursued unnatural desire, serve as an example by undergoing a punishment of eternal fire." Sodom was notorious as a city of sin, a place where unnatural desires ran wild. A modern-day comparison might be San Francisco. Jesus is saying, "You people think that Sodom is going to be punished for its immorality? That's nothing compared to what you unbelieving covenant people are facing if you do not repent and believe."

Let me put it bluntly: Jesus is saying that there is a sin far worse than sodomy. There is something far worse in God's eyes than homosexual behaviour. It is being a covenant child and then living in unbelief. Much worse than living a homosexual lifestyle is being a covenant member and then living in sin, never repenting, never turning. Such a person will receive far harsher treatment at the last judgment. God has a special measure of wrath in store for those who hear his promises and then spurn them, slapping him in the face.

You sometimes hear of Christian parents fretting over their kids and whether or not they might turn out gay, as if that would be the worst thing that could possibly happen. What Jesus says in Matthew 11 should be of far greater concern to Christian parents. A Christian who experiences same-sex attraction can fight that.[7] They must be encouraged to fight that. As they do, they can be a true child of God living out of faith in Jesus Christ. They can be heaven-bound because of God's gospel promises. It is not the end of the world. Christian parents should be far more concerned about what their children are doing with the promises of the covenant. If you are a parent, you should be praying constantly that your children be given the gift of faith so that they embrace those promises. You should be praying that none of your children will be a hypocrite or an

---

7. A helpful book on this subject is Sam Allberry's *Is God anti-gay? And other questions about homosexuality, the Bible, and same-sex attraction* (Epsom, UK: The Good Book Company, 2013).

unbeliever and fall under the dreadful curses of the covenant. You should pray that their baptism will not testify against them in the Day of Judgment.

You see, there is a way of death in the covenant of grace. If you refuse the LORD, it is not as though he turns away from you and just walks away. He takes it personally when you slap him in the face with unbelief – and well he should. You would expect a just God to do exactly that. Yet he is also a loving God. In his love, God holds out these warnings to his children. He says, "Don't go in the way of unbelief. Don't even flirt with it. It is the way of death; stay far away from it." That is what a loving Father does. He warns his children about danger. He even threatens them, "If you go down that path, there's a cliff and it's going to be your ruin. That way will destroy you forever." Listen to his warnings. Turn from the way of death to the way of life within the covenant of grace.

The Way to Life and Blessing

He wants all of us to do that and keep on doing that. He wants us to see the better way of relating to him in the covenant of grace and pursue that way. It is the way where you say, "Yes, he is my God and I am his child, part of his people. He is bound to me in love and I am bound to him in love." It is the way of faith and blessing.

If we think back to Lord's Day 31 again for a moment, we see this way described in QA 84, especially in the first paragraph:

> According to the command of Christ, the kingdom of heaven is opened when it is proclaimed and publicly testified to each and every believer that God has really forgiven all their sins for the sake of Christ's merits, as often as they by true faith accept the promise of the gospel...

When the gospel is preached, there is to be an announcement that whoever believes will have all their sins forgiven. When you by true faith accept the promise of the gospel, you receive all that is promised in the covenant of grace. When a believer sits in church and hears God's Word and says, "Yes, that's my God, that's my Saviour. I believe in him, I trust him, I love him, I want to submit to him," then that is indeed the way of life and blessing in the covenant of grace.

There are incentives drawing us to this way of life. In the Bible, God has many different ways of making the way of life attractive to us. He wants us to see that this is the better way and then respond accordingly. So, what are some of those incentives drawing us to faith in God within the covenant of grace?

We can begin with forgiveness (Colossians 1:14). What could be more important than being forgiven by God? When you know that you have offended him in every possible way, what could you long for more than forgiveness? In the covenant of grace, there is forgiveness when you believe God's promises. It is a promise that God is not going to hold your sins against you – ever! Forgiveness results in reconciliation. Reconciliation means peace with your holy, almighty and just Creator. The way of faith holds out peace to you. You can have the full assurance of peace both outwardly with God **and** inwardly in your conscience.

In that peace, you can not only live out your days, but you can also face physical death. You can face death without fear of what comes afterwards (1 Corinthians 15:56). The way of faith promises the blessing of a peaceful death. You can leave this world knowing that you are safe in Christ – no fear of judgment. Imagine one day being on your death-bed. Perhaps you will still be conscious and be able to speak to your family and friends. If so, you can assure them of your confidence in Christ. Think of how encouraging it would be for your loved ones to hear you affirm that your death is not a payment for sin, but it puts an end to sin and is an entrance into eternal life. This will be all because of Jesus, the Mediator of the covenant. The way of life in the covenant of grace makes all the difference at that crucial moment. It is the difference between a family comforted in your absence and a family left with questions and doubts. Faith gives a whole different perspective to the death of a Christian, a healthy and enriching perspective. In the way of life, the Christian can boldly say with Paul in Philippians 1:21, "For to me to live is Christ, and to die is gain."

So there is peace in life and death for the Christian who relates to God with faith in the context of the covenant of grace. There is also an abiding sense of joy. This is not the superficial happy-face type emotion. It is something that runs far deeper. It is an unshakable satisfaction in God, knowing that you are his beloved child and he is your God.

There once was this man who had been a slave to sexual sin. His mother Monica was a Christian and she had tried to lead her son to the gospel, but to no avail. Her son broke her heart with his unbelief. He was now 31 years old and living life his way. He had been co-habiting with a woman for several years. There he was one day in a garden in Milan, Italy when his eyes were miraculously opened by the Spirit. He was finally subdued by God and brought to the way of life in the covenant of grace. Who was this man? One of the greatest theologians in the history of the Christian church: Augustine of Hippo. He later wrote about this in his book, *Confessions*. He wrote,

> How sweet all at once it was for me to be rid of those fruitless joys which I had once feared to lose…! You drove them from me, you who are the true, the sovereign joy. You drove them from me and took their place, you who are sweeter than all pleasure…O Lord my God, my Light, my Wealth, and my Salvation.[8]

Augustine came to know the joy that comes from the way of life, the way of faith in God within the covenant of grace. God holds out that same joy to you as an incentive. He says, "Come live with me in this relationship, and I will be your joy." David says in Psalm 4:7, "You have put more joy in my heart than they have when their grain and wine abound." David knew the deep joy of living with God in faith.

8. *The Confessions of St. Augustine* (Westwood: The Christian Library, 1984), 138-139.

David also knew what it was to be chastised or disciplined by God. We do not normally think of discipline as a good and positive thing. It is somewhat counter-intuitive to regard discipline as an incentive to the way of life in the covenant of grace. Yet if we look at it in the light of what Hebrews 12 says, we should look at it as an incentive. When we take hold of the LORD's promises by faith and live within the covenant of grace, we have the promise of God's fatherly love. This is a love that will not let you go. This is a love that will not let you go on in sin and destroy yourself. According to Hebrews 12, God treats us as sons, and that means that he disciplines us and this is a good and desirable thing. At the moment you get it, discipline seems painful, "but later it yields the peaceful fruit of righteousness to those who have been trained by it" (Hebrews 12:11). Think about it: would you want a God who just let you go? No, if we reflect carefully on it, we want a God who cares enough about us to discipline us when we need it. He not only puts us on the way to life, he also keeps us there.

Another incentive to life in the covenant of grace has to do with following God's will. As we saw in the last chapter, true faith in Christ always bears fruit. Those who really believe in Christ want to obey God's law. They do not do it perfectly or constantly. The obedience of even the godliest Christians waxes and wanes, it goes in fits and starts. Yet the Holy Spirit does his work. Slowly and steadily, he leads believers to grow in holiness and Christ-likeness. This growing holiness is honouring to God. That is what we were created for. So the way of life gives that increasing sense of satisfaction that we are living the way we were created to.

There is more, because God promises that living in his ways is good for us. When you strive to follow God's will, it will be a blessing for you. It will not be a blessing in the sense of getting all kinds of material things or what have you. But it will be in the ways that really matter, such as our growing closer to the LORD, being better parents for our children, living in closer harmony with our neighbours in the world and brothers and sisters in the church, and so on. God's law is designed not only for his glory, but also for our good. That message is really driven home in the book of Proverbs. Wisdom and blessing can be expected to follow when believers submit to God's Word. It says in Proverbs 14:27, "The fear of the LORD is a fountain of life, that one may turn away from the snares of death." So faith leads to fruit, and fruit is glorifying to God and a blessing to us. That is another eminently good incentive to the way of life.

The Scriptures call you to embrace **life** in the covenant of grace. This is God's will for you. Another way of saying that is that you are called to believe God and all his promises. Hear what he holds out to you in Jesus Christ and embrace it for yourself. Then you will be relating to God in a wonderful way. He will be your heavenly Father who assures you every day of his love. He will be your Father who will someday take you into his blessed presence forever.

God's Word holds out to us these two ways: a way of death and a way of life. This is not an academic discussion of some fine theological point. What is on the table here is of enormous importance for each one of us. Eternity is at stake. There is a choice to be made. In Joshua 24, Joshua was addressing the covenant people of God as they were about to enter the Promised Land. There was a covenant renewal ceremony at Shechem. The people were pointedly challenged about their commitment to the LORD. Joshua told them, "Choose this day whom you will serve…" The choice was put before them: serve the LORD and live, or go back to paganism and die. Live with faith under the blessings of the covenant of grace, or be damned under its curses. Take your pick. The people insisted that they would follow the way of faith and live. This is what each one of us is called to do for ourselves: relate to God in the way of faith. It is the only way of life and blessings eternal.

Questions for Reflection and Discussion

1. Think of someone in Scripture who was a covenant member but chose the way of death. What led to that choice? How did that choice manifest itself? What consequences did this choice have? What else can we learn?

2. Why are some people (also believers) so resistant to speaking of warnings and threats within the covenant of grace?

3. What would you say to someone who says, "I can be serious about being a Christian later in life. Right now, I'm young and it's time to live it up. Besides, I belong to the covenant, so I have nothing to worry about"?

4. We saw some of the incentives to the way of life in the covenant of grace: forgiveness, peace in life and death, joy, discipline, and blessings which follow from obedience. Can you think of at least three other incentives that God holds forth in his Word?

5. Who magnifies the glory of God more: the unrepentant covenant breaker who goes the way of death or the repentant believer who goes the way of life? Explain your answer from Scripture.

CHAPTER FOUR – Our Children in the Covenant of Grace

Scripture: 1 Corinthians 7:1-16
Confessions: Heidelberg Catechism QA 74; Canons of Dort 1.17

We now want to begin looking at some of the ways in which this doctrine has a practical bearing on our lives. In this chapter we will look at how the covenant of grace relates to our children. In the next chapter, we will conclude by learning about how it directs our public worship.

We begin with our children. This brings us immediately to one of the most significant things that separate us from so many of the other church groups in our context. There are churches in North America that hold to the doctrines of grace like we do – by that, I mean that they hold to some or all of the so-called five points of Calvinism or TULIP. They might readily agree that unbelievers are dead in sin, utterly incapable of taking any steps toward God. With us, they might believe that God chose the elect unconditionally before the world was created, and so on. We can and we should rejoice that they exalt God when they hold to these biblical teachings. Yet at the same time, we have to be honest and recognize that there are key differences between us and them. Some of the most important differences have to do with the doctrine of the covenant of grace. This is not a minor or insignificant thing. What you believe about the covenant has an enormous bearing both on daily life as a Christian and on our life together as a church.

Certainly we should be able to agree that our children are important. We are not discussing whether pets go to heaven or something else relatively trivial. This is about our offspring, our flesh and blood, and how God relates to them. Our Baptistic friends might argue that God has little to do with them. There is nothing special about the children of believers as opposed to the children of unbelievers. However, because of our doctrine of the covenant of grace, we maintain that the children of believers are very special in the eyes of God. They are privileged, blessed, and have a distinct place in the church of Christ. Indeed, God in his Word assures us that all our children are included in the covenant of grace.

How We Consider Our Covenant Children

In this chapter, we are not going to get directly into the question of infant baptism.[9] Instead, we want to address the question behind the question. If our children belong to the covenant of grace, and if the sign and seal of entrance into the covenant is baptism, then, yes, obviously we should baptize our babies. But right now the fundamental question is: **do they belong to the covenant of grace, and if so, how?** What does it mean that they are covenant children and how should we then view them?

We must begin with the Old Testament administrations of the covenant of grace. When God made his covenant with Abraham in Genesis 17, this covenant was also established with Abraham's children. This was signified in the fact that all his male children were to receive circumcision. This was well-recognized by the Israelites because they continued this practice. They all knew full well that their children were covenant children. God had made his covenant not only with them, but also with their little ones.

There is no indication in Scripture that this changed with the coming of Christ. In Acts 2, Peter was preaching to Jewish people who had come from all over to Jerusalem. These were God's covenant people -- the males among them had each been circumcised. In Acts 2:39, Peter says those well-known words, "For the promise is for you and for your children and for all who are far off, everyone whom the Lord

9. For a helpful and concise treatment of this question, I highly recommend Daniel R. Hyde, *Jesus Loves the Little Children: Why We Baptize Children* (Grandville: Reformed Fellowship, Inc., 2006).

our God calls to himself." The promise is not only directed towards the adults, but also **to their children**. There is no indication in Scripture that membership in the covenant of grace became more restrictive after the coming of Christ.

Moreover, Hebrews 8:6 tells us that this new covenant administration after the coming of Christ is better. That should lead us to ask: how is a more restrictive covenant membership **better**? How is it **better** to leave the children of believers out? I have never seen a good answer to that question. There is no satisfactory answer to that question.

In fact, imagine if you were a Jewish parent living in the time of the apostles. Imagine if they were preaching the Baptist view, "Yes, I know that a couple of years ago, your children were included in God's covenant, but now that Jesus has come and done his work, they're out. Sorry!" As someone once said, a Jewish parent hearing that would probably think, "I thought this was supposed to be good news!" In Acts 15, we read about a controversy in the apostolic church about the application of the Mosaic ceremonial laws. If our Baptistic friends are right, would you not expect there to have been a similar controversy over the place of children in the covenant? Would you not expect to read about it in Scripture? However, Scripture says nothing and the silence indicates that on this point the New Testament church simply continued the Old Testament's inclusion of children. There is continuity on this point between the Old Testament and New Testament.

That brings us to this important passage from 1 Corinthians 7:12-16:

> [12] To the rest I say (I, not the Lord) that if any brother has a wife who is an unbeliever, and she consents to live with him, he should not divorce her. [13] If any woman has a husband who is an unbeliever, and he consents to live with her, she should not divorce him. [14] For the unbelieving husband is made holy because of his wife, and the unbelieving wife is made holy because of her husband. Otherwise your children would be

unclean, but as it is, they are holy. [15] But if the unbelieving partner separates, let it be so. In such cases the brother or sister is not enslaved. God has called you to peace. [16] For how do you know, wife, whether you will save your husband? Or how do you know, husband, whether you will save your wife?

Here Paul discusses a situation where you have a believer married to an unbeliever. That can be expected to happen in situations where people have come to the faith later in life. From elsewhere (e.g. 2 Corinthians 6:14ff.) we know that believers should only marry other believers, but this situation was different. These people were unbelievers when they got married, and then one of them became a Christian later. Paul uses covenantal language to indicate that this has a bearing on the status of the unbeliever in the marriage relationship. He speaks about being made holy or sanctified. This is covenantal language because God's covenant relationship is what sets people apart, which is what "holiness" essentially means. We could get into a discussion here of the covenant status of an unbeliever married to a believer, but that would take us down a rabbit trail. Here we want to focus on what Paul says at the end of 1 Corinthians 7:14. He tells us that the child of even just one believer is holy, set apart, sanctified. Again, that kind of language is covenantal. It is not just that this child has a better chance of becoming a Christian because he or she has a Christian parent. As true as that may be, there is far more here than that.

In Exodus 19, Israel was at Mount Sinai and God was establishing another administration of the covenant of grace. That is where he said that, within this covenant relationship, Israel would be to him "a kingdom of priests and a holy nation." In the Bible, holiness is something that exists within the framework of the covenant and it is the same here in 1 Corinthians 7. When Paul says that the children of believers are holy, he means to say that they are covenant children. Elsewhere he treats them like covenant children. Think of Ephesians 6:1-3 and how Paul addresses the children in the Ephesian church:

Children, obey your parents in the Lord, for this is right. [2] "Honor your father and mother" (this is the first commandment with a promise), [3] "that it may go well with you and that you may live long in the land."

The Ephesian children are addressed on the basis of God's covenant with God's law. That can only happen because they really are covenant children.

On that basis, today we do not consider our children to be little heathens or as someone once put it, "vipers in diapers." Yes, all our children need to be regenerated, and they all need to believe the promises of the gospel for themselves in due time, but yet they are all covenant children and they have a special status. As Lord's Day 27 puts it, they are distinguished from the children of unbelievers and their baptism publically announces that.

Our Form for Infant Baptism says that they are "sanctified in Christ." You find that in the first question to the parents. We are asked there, "Do you confess that our children are sanctified in Christ?" That expression has been debated vigorously in our Reformed church history. What does it mean that our children are "sanctified in Christ"? I am not going to review here all the different answers that have been given.[10] Remember: we want to keep this as an easy introduction to the doctrine of the covenant of grace. With that in mind, let me just briefly tell you what I think the best answer is. It means that they are in the covenant of grace, distinguished from the world, and entitled to all the benefits of Christ. God has promised those benefits to them, but to receive those benefits, they are each personally called to faith. "Sanctified in Christ" means that they have a standing in God's covenant of grace, but it does not mean that they will necessarily relate to God with faith and come under all the blessings and eternal life in the covenant of grace. There is still the call to faith for each and every child in the covenant. That

---

10. A good starting place for those interested would be chapter 5 of J. Kamphuis, *An Everlasting Covenant* (Launceston: Publication Organization of the Free Reformed Churches of Australia, 1985).

call is all the more urgent because of the very fact that they are "sanctified in Christ." Their covenant status means that they are more privileged, but also far more accountable for what they do with their privileges. We always ought to remember what Christ says in Luke 12:48, "Everyone to whom much was given, of him much will be required..." Greater riches and promises entail greater responsibility. That is a biblical principle.

How We Concretely Raise Our Covenant Children

These spiritual truths must have a concrete impact on how we raise our children. Let us look at some of the ways. At home, as we talk to our children, we must teach them that they have been given rich gospel promises by our God. We must explain those promises, how beautiful they are, how rich, and how much good news. As soon as they can understand, we begin telling them about their baptism and what it means. From their youngest days, we tell them that baptism means that they have been claimed by God to be his child. We teach them to understand that claim, accept it, believe it, and then live accordingly. In other words, we disciple our children, we shepherd them. We raise them in the ways of the Lord; we raise them to be Christians.

In many churches, they have special youth pastors. So do confessionally Reformed churches like ours. We actually have a whole army of youth pastors in our churches. They are called parents. Parents are the front-line youth pastors in a Reformed church. Parents, your calling is to do what you promised to do at the baptism of your children: "instruct your child in this doctrine, as soon as he or she is able to understand, and to have him or her instructed therein to the utmost of your power". Dear reader, if you are a parent, I want to urge you to take that calling seriously. It is **your** calling first and foremost, not the church through catechism classes or the teachers at the Christian school. It is **your** calling to disciple and shepherd the children God has entrusted to you.

Yet, having made that point, no one should think that Christian education is then optional for Reformed believers. We find this emphasized in article 58 of our Church Order:

> The consistory shall ensure that the parents, to the best of their ability, have their children attend a school where the instruction given is in harmony with the Word of God as the church has summarized it in her confessions.

Here our churches have agreed that consistories shall pay attention to what is happening with the education of our covenant children. The elders have a responsibility to ensure that, as much as possible, the covenant children of each congregation are being taught in a way that not only does not conflict with what the church teaches, but which actually harmonizes with what the church teaches. This article in our Church Order follows article 57 about baptism. There is a good and biblical reason for that. Christian education follows from the covenant status of our children. Let me be clear: that does not begin with the consistory breathing down your neck about it. That begins with you being convinced in your heart as a Christian parent that your child has a special covenant status from which necessarily follows a Christian education. At our Christian schools, if they are functioning as they should, your child will be educated in a way that fits with their position in the covenant of grace. That is just not going to happen in a public school. While there might yet be individual Christians teaching within the public system, it is a system dominated by a worldly and anti-Christian philosophy of education from the earliest levels to the highest. We want our children to honour God and acknowledge him in all their ways from their youngest years. Therefore, faithful parents of covenant children will always place enormous value on Christian education and even make great sacrifices to make it happen.

There is another important impact of our children's place in the covenant and that has to do with the church. As participants in the covenant of grace, we believe that all our children are members of the church of Christ. They are not potential members or "members-in-training". All our children, even the very youngest, are members of our churches. Sometimes there is this mistaken notion that our children become members when they do public profession of faith. This is simply **not** true. Our children become members when they come into the covenant of grace, which is to say, from the moment they are conceived in their mother's womb. What happens at public profession of faith is not membership in the church, but a shift from being a non-communicant member to being a communicant member. At public profession of faith, our children take responsibility for their church membership. Yet they have **always** been members of the church. That is an important point of difference with so many around us. So many Christians today do not look at their children as being members of the church. This is not a theoretical question -- it has a practical bearing.

One crucial place the practical bearing comes into play is public worship. If the kids are not members, then they do not really belong in public worship. They do not understand anything anyway; they are not going to get anything out of it and they cannot contribute much, if anything, to it. Therefore, instead of meeting with God along with the adults, the kids can and should go to some program designed especially for them. This is what inevitably follows from restricting the covenant and church membership to believers only.

We take a different approach and we always have. Children belong to the church, therefore they belong in public worship as soon as possible. They belong in that covenant meeting between God and his people, because they are part of God's people. To leave them out would be to say that the call to worship for God's people does not apply to them. If we are consistent with following through on our covenant theology, that would be unthinkable.

There was that occasion in Mark 10 where the disciples tried to keep those covenant children away from Jesus. The disciples thought that Jesus was far too important for these little ones. Scripture says in Mark 10:14 that when Jesus saw this he became indignant. It infuriated him that his disciples would restrict these little covenant people from having access to him. Then he took these little people in his arms, he hugged them and blessed them. Our Lord Jesus is not here today on earth to hug the little brothers and sisters, but he is still here to bless them, too, whenever we worship. It would make Jesus indignant for anyone to keep them away. Our covenant children belong to the church and they belong in our worship services. Indeed, still today we can say, "Let the little children come to Jesus, do not hinder them!"

As soon as they are able, we want to see our covenant children meeting with their God. "As soon as they are able" means that there is going to be some variation and we cannot set a hard and fast rule about it. Some children are squirmier than others. I get that -- I have kids too. Some kids come into this world naturally more docile and they can sit in church when they are two. Other kids are going to take a little while longer and that is perfectly okay. Yet they all belong there eventually. There are going to be some challenges that come along with that. Sometimes kids learning to come to church are going to make some noise and be a bit restless. The rest of us in the covenant community have to cut parents and kids some slack; be patient, and just rejoice that the kids are there. Let the little children come! They belong with us in God's presence, all of them. God is present to bless them as well as us.

As parents, there are some things we need to do to make that happen. From as soon as they are able to understand, we start teaching them about what church is and what we are doing when we gather for worship. This is part of discipleship. We teach them to be respectful and reverent in church. When they are able to read, we make sure they have a Bible and a Book of Praise. We make sure they start following along and that they are singing with the rest of the congregation. We teach them to do these things from when they are young. We do not tell them it is optional, that you can sing if you feel like it. No, we are all part of God's covenant people and so we all sing together, young and old, good singers and not-so-good singers. When the collection comes, we have to make sure that our kids are actively participating in that element of our worship too. They can put money in the collection. That is part of worship too, something they can easily do to worship the LORD. Moreover, what about the sermon? Many times, the minister will work the kids into the sermon. Parents of covenant children should follow up on that and make sure their kids understand. God's Word is for them too. You can often be surprised what kids pick up and we should encourage them to be listening to God's Word as it is preached. It is for them too, as they are also being addressed as part of God's covenant people.

The Comfort We Have When Covenant Children Die

The last area where our covenant theology makes a huge difference is the comfort we have should we lose them our covenant children. That can happen. It has happened to many of us. Many of us have lost covenant children before they ever took a breath outside the womb. Some of us have lost covenant children after they were born, too. All these losses are painful. When you have a little child, you love that child and you have hopes and dreams for him or her. An early infant loss can be a really difficult thing to go through, both for moms and dads.[11]

It is quite remarkable that this type of situation is explicitly addressed in our confessions. We often think of the Heidelberg Catechism as the confession of comfort. However, it is not the Catechism that speaks about this. Instead, we find it in the Canons of Dort. The Canons speak about the doctrines of grace and that includes the comfort that parents of covenant children can have when those children die in infancy:

> We must judge concerning the will of God from His Word, which declares that the children of believers are holy, not by nature but in virtue of the covenant of grace, in which they are included with their parents. Therefore, God-fearing parents ought not to doubt the election and salvation of their children whom God calls out of this life in their infancy.

This was written at a time when infant mortality was far higher than what we see today. Many of us have experienced early infant loss, but not nearly anywhere on the scale of what people would have

---

11. An excellent book on this subject is Glenda Mathes, *Little One Lost: Living with Early Infant Loss* (Grandville: Reformed Fellowship, Inc., 2012).

experienced in the 1600s. Far fewer children lived to be adults in those days. Many died of diseases that are today easily treated or vaccinated against. The vast majority of Reformed parents would have experienced not only miscarriage, but even more likely, the death of a young child after birth. What does God's Word say to that? What can pastors say to parents grieving in those circumstances?

Our confession reminds us of what we have already covered: our children are holy because they are in the covenant of grace with their parents. When such children are taken out of this world in their infancy, there is no need for Christian parents to doubt their final destiny. We need not be wondering about their election and salvation. In fact, we can be confident of the Lord's mercy and grace towards them. We can be like David in 2 Samuel 12. When the little child died who had been conceived in that adulterous relationship with Bathsheba, David expressed his confidence that this child went to be with God. He said in 2 Samuel 12:23, "I shall go to him, but he will not return to me." David was sure that when he died, he would be reunited with his son. That solid confidence comes from the covenant of grace that God makes with believers **and** their children.

Reflecting on this further, you might ask, "How does God relate to those in the covenant of grace who are presently unable to relate to him?" An infant child cannot respond to God's promises. Of course, children are only able to do that as they get older, as they reach an age of responsibility (an age which varies from child to child). Some children never make it to such an age of accountability. Additionally, there are not only children, we could also think of those with intellectual disabilities. Sometimes an intellectual disability in a covenant child can be so severe that they are not able at all to relate to God in a responsible way. They are simply not able to respond to God's gospel promises the way the rest of us might and should. So what does God do with them? Did we not learn in the last chapters that there is nothing automatic in the covenant of grace? Does this contradict that? No, not at all.

There can be, and are, individuals in the covenant of grace who cannot relate to God, who cannot respond to his overtures towards them. Yet God mercifully relates to them through their covenant heads. They are in the covenant because of their relationship to a believer. The children of believers are holy because their parents are believers. Their parents are their covenant heads – particularly the father if he is a believer. The man is the covenant head of not only his wife, but also of his whole family. God relates to the children too through their covenant head. If their parents are believers in the gospel promises, and if that child is taken out of this world before he or she could respond to those gospel promises personally, then God views that child through the parents. In his grace, he regards that child as he would a believer who embraced Christ. No one comes to heaven apart from faith in Christ, and that includes covenant children. Even with them, it is not automatic. There is no salvation for anyone apart from faith in Jesus Christ. For covenant children who die in infancy, it is the faith of their parents that makes the difference.

What a comfort that gives us when we face the tragedy of early infant loss! Our children belong to the LORD and if they are called out of this life in infancy, in his grace he takes them to himself. That little child you lost is now in the presence of God, praising him along with the holy angels. That little child you lost – that was not a short life wasted. That was not a pointless loss. God took your child directly to himself and that child did not have to bear the brokenness of a world under the curse. That child is fulfilling God's purpose for him or her, exalting our Father right now. It was a loss to you, and death is an enemy, also when it comes to our kids. Yet here too we can say that Christ has conquered death and removed its sting. We can have comfort, because we have this covenant theology from the Scriptures; we are taught that God has a covenant of grace that includes believers **and** their offspring.

I want you to see how rich we are with these gospel truths. The covenant of grace shows us a God who loves us **and** our children. He has always included the children with his people and there is no reason to think that he stopped doing that after Christ came and died for us. So, let me ask you, why would you ever want to trade in these truths for something less? Why would you settle for a gospel that is not covenantal? The gospel that is good news is good news not only for us, but also for our dear children.

Questions for Reflection and Discussion

1. Does the covenant status of our children mean that we should presume that they have each been born again or regenerated? Explain your answer with Scripture.

2. Paedo-communion teaches that all covenant children should be able to partake in the Lord's Supper. Part of the argument is that we do not deny them one sacrament (baptism), so we should not deny them the other sacrament. How would you respond to that view?

3. Can you think of a believer in the New Testament who was apparently discipled from a young age within the covenantal family setting? What lessons might be taken from what Scripture reveals about this?

4. Canons of Dort 1.17 speaks clearly about the infant children of believers. What can we say on the basis of Scripture about the children of unbelievers who die in infancy?

5. Some say that we should send our covenant children to public schools so that they can be a salt and light, so that they can witness for Christ, and also learn how to defend their faith. How should we evaluate that position?

CHAPTER FIVE - The Covenant of Grace and Public Worship

Scripture: Leviticus 10:1-11, Malachi 1
Confessions: Heidelberg Catechism QA 96

In the last chapter, we learned how the covenant of grace concretely impacts the way we view our children. We also learned that it affects the way we raise our children. For instance, we saw that it is our children's place in the covenant of grace that leads us to insist that they always have a place with us in public worship. As soon as they are able, we want them to be with us meeting with our covenant God in worship.

Worship is what we are focussing on in this final chapter. What difference does a Reformed doctrine of the covenant of grace make when it comes to our worship? We are going to see that it makes **a lot** of difference. It is what explains why our worship services are so different from other church groups around us, even those who might hold to the doctrines of grace like we do.

Sometimes the differences between us and others are chalked up to mere differences in taste. One church has a more "contemporary" worship style, and another church has a more "traditional" worship style. It is similar to the way that you like rice, whereas I like potatoes. Or you say 'tomahto', and I say 'tomayto'. So for some it becomes just a matter of preference. We are told that it is merely a subjective thing. If that is true, then it really makes no difference. We are all worshipping God, and we all do it in equally legitimate ways. But is this really true? Can we just worship God however we want and then defend ourselves by saying it is just a matter of preference?

If you are paying attention, you will invariably hear about all kinds of things going on in worship services around us. There are the churches that incorporate yoga into their service. There are those who have puppet shows or stage performances including dancers or musicians. There was a Christian Reformed church in Calgary some years ago that made the news when their pastor started preaching a series of sermons on the TV show 'the Simpsons.' For some Sundays they would sit and watch an episode of 'the Simpsons' and then the pastor would preach his sermon on that, instead of on the Bible. He reasoned that God reveals himself in popular culture too, so why not listen to what God is saying in 'the Simpsons.'[12] Is it really just a matter of preference? You prefer a sermon on the Bible, and I prefer a sermon on 'the Simpsons'? Is that just a different worship style that we are not used to? Or is there something more going on?

There is indeed something more going on -- a lot more! It has everything to do with the covenant of grace and how we understand it. In this chapter, we are going to learn how the Bible's doctrine of the covenant of grace makes Reformed worship distinct.

The Essence of Reformed Worship

In the first chapter, one of the first things we learned was that the covenant of grace is essentially the relationship that God has with his people. There is a bond between the LORD and, not only believers, but also believers and their children. This relationship impacts everything in the lives of Christians, including how we worship.

We also saw earlier that the covenant relationship between God and his people is often compared in Scripture to a marriage. If we read books like Ezekiel and Hosea, we see God as a husband complaining about the unfaithfulness of his wife. The marriage relationship was not working the way that it should. It was an unhealthy relationship – there was dysfunction and brokenness. We expect to see certain things in a healthy marriage relationship. For example, we would expect to see husband and wife communicating with one another;

12. See my article, "The Gospel According to Bart Simpson?" in *Clarion* 50.5 (March 2, 2001), 109-110.

to see them engaging each other in dialogue. In a healthy marriage, one partner does not do all the talking while the other just sits and listens – there should be back and forth.

That was the pattern of Old Testament worship. The Israelites did not invent the tabernacle or temple worship. What was done at the tabernacle (and later the temple) was ordained by God himself. It was revealed in the Law. In the Old Testament, when God's people were faithful and worshipping according to his Word, what was happening at the sanctuary reflected the relationship between God and his people. There was back and forth between God and his people, just as you would expect to see in a properly functioning relationship. God was present at the tabernacle as the people gathered. He was present in a special way to bless his people. The people were there to bring their sacrifices, songs, and prayers. The sacrifices were presented through the mediation of the priests. At certain points in the tabernacle liturgy, the priests represented God and what he was saying and doing. At other points, the priests represented the people and what they were saying and doing. Through it all, there was a back and forth. There was movement in the tabernacle.[13] Moreover, it all pointed ahead to our Saviour Jesus Christ. At the same time, everything said "relationship."

In the New Testament, we no longer have a temple or tabernacle like they did in the Old Testament. Christ is in heaven, in the real holy of holies. The gospel proclaims that he has made the sacrifice for our sin that has turned away the wrath of God and returned his favour. Through Christ's suffering and death on the cross we have reconciliation with the holy God. Therefore, sacrifices for sin are no longer needed and indeed, the whole ceremonial system has been fulfilled. Yet God still calls his people to worship him and he promises to be there to bless them when they gather. This is an important point.

---

13. This is explained in more detail by G. Van Dooren in, *The Beauty of Reformed Liturgy* (Winnipeg: Premier Publishing, 1980), 16-20.

There are those who say that there is nothing really special about believers gathering together for worship. Some say that God is present everywhere, so we do not need to go to church to worship him. God is present in Algonquin Park, so I can take my canoe and go to Algonquin Park on Sunday and worship him there instead. Why not? Here is why not: because God does not promise to bless you with the Word and sacraments in Algonquin Park. He is present there, but in public worship, when God's people gather together around the means of grace, he is present in a special way. In fact, it is so special that the apostle Paul says in 1 Corinthians 3:16-17 that the church (not the building, but the people) is the temple of God. Peter says the same thing in 1 Peter 2:5. The church is a spiritual house, a place for the offering of spiritual sacrifices. The church is the New Testament temple. God promised to be present to bless his people at the Old Testament temple; now he also promises to be present to bless his people at the New Testament temple, when the church is gathered together before him to receive the ministry of the Word and sacraments.

So the Bible teaches that God is present in a special way when his people are gathered together in obedience to his call. That meeting must reflect the relationship that God has with his people. It must reflect the covenant. So there must be a back and forth; there must be two-way communication in the worship service. It cannot be a monologue, with only us speaking to God all the time. Flipping it around, it cannot be God only speaking to us all the time. Our service must reflect a relationship between two parties and a properly functioning relationship is going to have communication, dialogue, back and forth. The essence of Reformed worship is that it reflects the covenant relationship between God and his people.

Moreover, we must always remember that this is not a relationship between equals. God is the one who is infinitely greater in the covenant of grace. God is the one who has graciously initiated this relationship. God is the one who has called us into his presence. God is sovereign and holy. Since all these things are true, we recognize that God alone has the right to determine the terms by which we will have this worship conversation or dialogue. We do not decide what is and is not appropriate. We do not have that prerogative. Because of who God is in relation to us, in the covenant of grace, we must leave it to him to determine what we shall do and what we shall say.

Accordingly, this is what we confess in QA 96 of the Catechism:

Q. What does God require in the second commandment?

A. We are not to make an image of God in any way, nor to worship Him in any other manner than He has commanded in His Word.

This is about the second Word of the covenant: "You shall not make for yourself a carved image, or any likeness of anything…" We confess that we are to worship God in no other way than he has commanded in his Word. We call that **the regulative principle of worship**.[14] It is the application of *Sola Scriptura* (by Scripture alone) to our worship. We do not decide how to worship God on our own. Please note: this is far different from the way many other Christians worship. For most other Christians, the principle is that if the Bible does not forbid it, then you can do it. That is what can lead to some strange worship practices. The Bible does not forbid yoga in the worship service, so you can do it. No, we say, we only worship God as he has commanded. He has not commanded us to do yoga, so we do not do yoga. Or take what I mentioned earlier about 'the Simpsons.' The popular approach says, "God does not forbid watching 'the Simpsons' on a big screen in church on Sunday morning, so we can do it." No, we say, we only worship God as he has commanded. We do not add or take away from his commands. He has not commanded us to replace the reading and preaching of Scripture with the watching and preaching of 'the Simpsons' so we simply do not do it. The regulative principle of worship is a

---

14. The regulative principle is also found in articles 7 and 32 of the Belgic Confession. See my *The Whole Manner of Worship: Worship and the Sufficiency of Scripture in Belgic Confession Article 7* (Edmonton: Still Waters Revival Books, 1997).

safeguard against all kinds of deviations and departures.

Our covenant God takes worship very seriously and so should we. We see that powerfully illustrated in this passage from Leviticus 10:

> Now Nadab and Abihu, the sons of Aaron, each took his censer and put fire in it and laid incense on it and offered unauthorized fire before the LORD, which he had not commanded them. [2] And fire came out from before the LORD and consumed them, and they died before the LORD. [3] Then Moses said to Aaron, "This is what the LORD has said: 'Among those who are near me I will be sanctified, and before all the people I will be glorified.'" And Aaron held his peace.

Nadab and Abihu offered "unauthorized fire" before the LORD. The details of what that involved are not clear. What is clear is that they were attempting to worship God in a way that had not been authorized. Things did not turn out well for Nadab and Abihu. However well-intentioned they may have been, God was not pleased with their worship -- quite the opposite! They learned the hard way that the holy covenant God is a consuming fire (Hebrews 12:28-29). They were to worship God only as he commanded and so are we. The Second Commandment is still in force for us today as Christians and we have to honour it. As Christians redeemed by Christ, would we not **want** to honour it? Why would a believer bought with the blood of Christ strike off on his or her own and say, "Forget it, God, I know you loved me so much that you sent your Son to die for my sins, but I want to worship you my way." Surely that would be absurd. Jesus was clear on this in John 14:15, "If you love me, you will keep my commandments." Those who love Christ and have true faith in him bear the fruits of faith in a life that wants to follow God's ways, also when it comes to worship.

The Elements of Reformed Worship

That brings us to consider what exactly God has commanded for Christian worship. If he is the lead party in the covenant of grace, what has he laid out as the elements of our meeting with him? It is really quite simple. God has commanded the reading and preaching of Scripture (2 Timothy 4:2). There is prayer (1 Timothy 2:8). There is the giving of Christian alms, the giving of offerings for the needy (Deuteronomy 16:17; 1 Corinthians 16:1-2). There is the singing of psalms and hymns (Ephesians 5:19; Colossians 3:16). There is the administration of the sacraments of baptism and the Lord's Supper (Matthew 28:19; 1 Corinthians 11:23-26). On some occasions (e.g. profession of faith, ordination/installation of office bearers), there is also the making of vows before the LORD and his people – something found in both the Old and the New Testament (see Lord's Day 37 of the Heidelberg Catechism). Those are the divinely commanded elements of worship and we dare not add or subtract from them.

But perhaps this raises some questions in your mind. What about when we worship? Or the musical instruments we use in our worship? There is an important distinction we need to know in order to answer these questions responsibly. We have to distinguish **elements** of worship from **circumstances** of worship. Elements are the things commanded in God's Word: preaching, singing, praying, etc. The regulative principle of worship governs the elements. Circumstances are things surrounding the elements, things that are incidental. For example, we might worship at 9:30 AM and 3:30 PM. God's Word does not command these precise times. In fact, we have the freedom to determine the times at which we will worship on the Lord's Day. Consistories must use wisdom informed by God's Word to decide on these times. Of course, part of wisdom means also taking into account the circumstances of the congregation. The types of musical instruments we use are also not commanded in Scripture. It is not required that we use an organ or a piano, or even any instrument at all. Many of our Brazilian brothers and sisters worship every Sunday without any musical accompaniment and that is acceptable too. The instrument and the choice of instrument are incidental – the musical accompaniment is there to support and enhance the singing. These things are circumstances and therefore not governed by the regulative principle.

Perhaps there are other questions. Maybe someone looks over our typical order of worship and says, "If there are only to be those elements of worship you mentioned, how do you explain things like the Votum, and the Salutation, and the Ten Commandments?" To answer that, have you noticed that all of those elements involve Scripture? They fall under the reading of Scripture. Scripture is used not only at the opening of our worship services, but throughout. In fact, it is another distinctive feature of Reformed worship: the Bible is there, open, and being used from beginning to end. Even in our singing! Most of our singing is done directly from God's Word, from the Psalms and from hymns that are based on Scripture. This is one of the richest parts of our Reformed heritage and it often strikes visitors who have not grown up with it.

So God's position in the covenant of grace impacts our worship because he alone can determine what we do in worship. We have these divinely commanded elements. But how should these elements be structured in the order of worship? That is also where the covenant plays a role.

The Structure of Reformed Worship

If we look at the elements, there is something that points us in the direction we should go here. Some of the elements come from our side. For instance, we pray, we make offerings, we sing. There are other elements that come from God's side. God speaks his Word to us through the reading of Scripture and the preaching. There are a few things that follow from this.

The basic structure of our worship is going to reflect the covenant relationship between God and his people. There are the elements from man's side and from God's side and they should be put together in a way that reflects a covenant dialogue. There should be a back and forth between God and his people through the course of a service. That is what we see in a typical Reformed order of worship. We see this pattern: God speaks, his people respond. So, for example, there should be a call to worship at the beginning – that is God speaking. His people respond with the votum from Psalm

124:8. Then God speaks the words of greeting and blessing in the salutation. Then we respond with a song of praise. On it goes through the course of the entire service, back and forth.

What about the beginning and end of the service? How should that be done? If our worship is connected to the covenant of grace, and if God is the one who has the first word in the covenant of grace, would it not make sense that he must have the first word in the service? God initiates the covenant of grace. He has the first word there. That is why Reformed worship services should begin with a call to worship. The service does not begin with the handshake. It does not begin with the votum. Our meeting with God begins when he says it does, with his Word. Likewise, it ends with his Word. Our covenant God sends us away with his blessing in the benediction. He has the first word in our worship and he has the last word.

He is also at the center of the service with the ministry of the Word and sacraments. Again, that reflects his exalted position in the covenant of grace. When you look around, it often seems that people think that the center of worship is us and what we are doing for God in this hour of meeting with him. I once watched a service which began with 45 minutes of singing and then the music leader said, "Now that the worship is over, we'll listen to a message from Pastor Dave." That gives the impression that the real center of the service is us and our singing. That is **not** the biblical approach to worship. At the center of the service is God and what he is doing. That is why in a Reformed worship service, the preaching of God's Word and the administration of the sacraments are always in the center. This is the high point, the climax of Reformed worship. It is God bringing his Word to us through one of his servants to create and nourish faith. It is God bringing the sacraments to us through one of his servants to strengthen our faith. These things are in the center, because God is in the center of the covenant of grace.

Intimately related to that is the place of Christ as the Mediator of the covenant of grace. We can only expect to come into God's presence through the mediation of Christ. In ourselves we have no right to approach the holy God. After all, we are great sinners. He is holy and by ourselves we are not. If we were to come as we are, we would die. Yet we have Christ and he makes all the difference. Through Christ's blood we are washed and cleaned up, not only for salvation, but also for worship and entrance into the presence of our great God. At the center of our worship, then, is a ministry of Word and sacrament which points to this Saviour. Every week God's people have to be reoriented to Jesus Christ and that is what has to happen at the center of a biblical worship service. This Jesus-centered focus is why preaching and the sacraments are in the limelight of a Reformed worship service. These things point to him. You see, it is not about us, but about him.

The Style of Reformed Worship

Seeing God as having the prime place in the covenant of grace is also going to dramatically impact and distinguish the style of Reformed worship. By "style," I mean things like our attitude towards worship, our dress and deportment, our church architecture, the way our music is played and sung, and so on. These are not trivial or indifferent matters. How we come into God's presence and how we conduct ourselves in God's presence matters tremendously.

We can learn that from Malachi 1, especially these words from verses 6-8:

> [6] "A son honors his father, and a servant his master. If then I am a father, where is my honor? And if I am a master, where is my fear? says the LORD of hosts to you, O priests, who despise my name. But you say, 'How have we despised your name?' [7] By offering polluted food upon my altar. But you say, 'How have we polluted you?' By saying that the LORD's table may be despised. [8] When you offer blind animals in sacrifice, is that not evil? And when you offer those that are lame or sick, is that not evil? Present that to your governor; will he accept you or show you favor? says the LORD of hosts.

In many of the books of the prophets we find God pressing a covenant lawsuit against his people. He has this relationship with them and they have violated the relationship. They have not believed the LORD and followed him and so he goes after them with his prophets and confronts them with their covenant breaking. In Malachi 1, he speaks about their worship. On a superficial level, it looked like the people were worshipping God faithfully, as he commanded. However, God saw what was really happening.

What was really happening was that the people were bringing sacrifices that were second-rate and thinking that God would not notice. After all, other people did not notice. So, for example, verse 8 says that the people were bringing blind animals for sacrifices. It would not be obvious to anyone else that the animal was blind. Yet God's law had expressly commanded that only the best sacrifices be brought to him (e.g. Leviticus 22:22). God wanted only the best and healthiest animals. Yet here the Israelites were trying to cut corners, offering God the weak and sick animals, thinking he would not notice. He noticed. Then he says in verse 8, "Try and do that with a human ruler. Bring your human ruler your weak and sick animals as a gift; try bringing him your second or third best. See if **he** would accept that!"

That teaches us an important principle about worship. Since God is exalted, because he has the number one place in the covenant relationship, because he is our God, we want to bring him only our absolute best. He is worthy of that. That applies to external things like how we dress when we come to church. Do we really believe that we are meeting in a special way with the most exalted King in the universe? Then that should be reflected in the way we dress. We do not want to draw up a dress code for the church, and we should not be looking at others. Each of us should ourselves be conscientious about this. Should we not offer **our very best** as we meet with the King of kings? That applies to everything. It applies also to our singing, to the playing of musical accompaniment, to the preparation of sermons, to the way we treat our church building, our attention to the sermon – in everything we want to offer our covenant God the absolute best when we worship. He deserves it. He is worthy of it.

Yet let us be clear: it is not just about the external things. The external things are not even the most important thing. The most important thing is what is going on in your heart, your attitude as you approach the Holy One of Israel. The first and foremost thing he desires is your heart, a heart that loves him and wants to glorify him. When our hearts have been made alive by the grace of God, when we see how much we have been loved by this exalted God, when we see what a treasure the covenant relationship is, that is inevitably going to have an impact on how we come to meet with this covenant God. That will shape our attitude: do we come into God's presence because we have to, or because we really want to?

To say it as clearly as possible: the style of our worship is going to reflect our understanding of whom this God is who has covenanted with us. Is he high and exalted, a majestic and transcendent God? Or do we think of him as a distant observer and not really present in our services? Or worse, do we think of him as a low-brow god who will always just take what he can get from us, even if it is second or third-best? Basically, do we accept and believe what God's Word says about himself and let that impact the manner and style of our meeting with him?

As we conclude, let us appreciate again the riches that we have as Reformed churches. We have a rich heritage of applying God's Word to worship, taking *Sola Scriptura* seriously also when we meet with God on Sunday. We do that because we take God seriously as our covenant God. He has approached us and called us his own. He says, "I am your God and you are my people." When he says, "I am your God," he means "I am number one for you. I have priority in this relationship; I alone determine how you will worship me." Since we are united to Christ, since his Spirit animates our hearts, we respond to these claims with eager and willing affirmation. Reformed believers have always acknowledged these truths and we should continue doing so. Other churches might offer a better worship "experience." Their music might be able to supply warm emotional moments. However, the Bible does not put these things in the center – the Bible does not put you in the center -- and so neither should we. If we follow the Bible, the center of Christian worship will be a pulpit, not a stage. Just as in the covenant, God stands central, God's Word stands central, and the gospel of Jesus Christ stands central. That is what makes Reformed worship distinctly different.

Questions for Reflection and Discussion

1. How does the singing of psalms reinforce the covenantal character of Reformed worship?

2. In the Old Testament, the prophets sometimes challenged God's covenant people by means of object lessons. For example, in Ezekiel 12, the prophet's actions symbolized Judah's captivity. How would you respond to those who argue that these object lessons justify the use of similar object lessons in public worship today?

3. Should there be any place for artistic creativity in Reformed covenantal worship? Why or why not?

4. What sorts of allowances can or should be made for making Reformed worship understandable or accessible to visitors who might not share our background? For example, would it be acceptable for the minister to explain briefly why we read the Ten Commandments each Sunday morning?

5. If we can watch a service online from the comfort of our own home, why should we bother to make the effort to travel to a public worship service in a church building? Does it really matter whether we are there in person?

Appendix – Seven Essential Distinctions in the Doctrine of the Covenant of Grace

Good distinctions are part of the essence of sound theology. They are an important tool for theologians. Preachers often employ distinctions as well, though because they can be technical, they are not always mentioned explicitly. In the preceding chapters, I have worked with the seven distinctions found below, even if I have not always mentioned them outright. Along with some brief explanation, they are included here for those readers who may be more theologically inclined.

We distinguish between the administration of the covenant of grace in this era and administrations of the covenant of grace in previous eras.
There is substantially one covenant of grace revealed in Scripture in both the Old and New Testaments. However, Reformed theology recognizes that this one covenant of grace has had several administrations. Each administration has its own character. For example, the covenant of grace as administered to Abraham contained a promise of offspring and land and involved a sign and seal of circumcision (Genesis 17:1-14). The covenant of grace as administered to believers and their children today contains the promises of the gospel in Jesus Christ and involves the sign and seal of baptism.

We distinguish between parties in the gracious covenant relationship: on the one side, God; on the other all believers with all their children. Jesus Christ mediates between these two parties.
Any covenant by definition has parties. In the covenant of grace, the Creator relates to certain creatures, namely with believers and

their children (Acts 2:39). However, for this relationship to function as intended, because it involves a Holy God and a sinful people, a Mediator is required and according to passages like Hebrews 8:6, Christ is that Mediator.

We distinguish between greater and lesser parties in the covenant of grace. God is the infinitely greater; his people the lesser. Therefore, God alone initiates this gracious relationship and determines its terms.

The Creator and the creature are not only distinct from one another in terms of their being (ontologically), they are also distinct in terms of their transcendence (qualitatively). With his great majesty, the Creator vastly transcends all human creatures (Psalm 145:3). This gets worked out historically as we observe God pursuing Adam in the first administration of the covenant of grace, Abraham in a subsequent, and still later the Israelites. Every administration of the covenant of grace sees God taking the initiative and determining the terms.

We distinguish between promises and obligations in the covenant of grace. God gives promises and imposes obligations (or conditions) in this relationship.

Promises and obligations are included in the essence of covenant relationships in Scripture. Without them, there would be no covenant relationship. Because of the preceding distinction, it is God who sovereignly determines what shall be promised and what shall be expected.

We distinguish between God extending the gospel promises and man receiving what is promised. God extends his gospel promises to all in the covenant of grace, but not all receive what is promised.

It cannot be said that all covenant members automatically receive what is promised. This is evident from examples in Scripture such as that of Esau. As a son of Isaac, he was included in an administration of the covenant of grace. Esau received circumcision, the sign and seal of that covenant administration. Yet Scripture says he failed to receive what was promised (Malachi 1:2-3).

We distinguish between antecedent and consequent conditions in the covenant of grace. The antecedent condition is a true faith which unites one to Christ and all his saving benefits. The consequent condition is the fruit of faith and union with Christ in a growing, holy obedience to God's law.

Justification and every other saving benefit promised in the gospel (promised in the covenant) can only be received through true faith (Romans 4). We do not and cannot earn our place in the covenant of grace. However, Scripture is abundantly clear that a true faith must inevitably (or consequently) produce good works, and if it does not, it is not a true faith (James 2:14-26). The relationship between these two is one of root and fruit.

We distinguish between two ways of relating to God within the covenant relationship: a strictly legal relation characterized by unbelief, which leads only to curse and death; a vital relation characterized by true faith, which leads to blessing and life.

Scripture speaks of those who break the covenant (e.g. Ezekiel 16:59). This language speaks of unfaithfulness and dysfunction within the covenant relationship – not the utter dissolution of this relationship. This unfaithfulness leads to consequences – first chastisement (discipline) and then later, if there is no repentance, just punishment. All wickedness will be punished by God, but he has a special measure of wrath for covenant breakers (Hebrews 10:26-31). He yet maintains a relationship with them, but it is a hostile one of Judge/accused or King/traitor. However, those who have true faith live in fellowship with him in the covenant relationship through the mediation of Jesus Christ. Through Christ, they enjoy a living, joyful, and healthy relationship, one of Father/son.

Further Study

Recommended for Further Study

For those who might be interested in learning more about covenant theology, I have compiled this list, along with some brief comments about each item. The list is not comprehensive, and they are not given in any particular order. Mentioning them does not mean that I agree with every single detail, term, or formulation in them — indeed, some of them contradict each other at certain points. In sharing them here, all I mean to say is that I have learned something valuable from them and perhaps you can too.

The Covenant of Grace, John Murray (Phillipsburg: P&R, 1953, 1988).

This is a dense little booklet of 32 pages. Murray explains quite well the idea of different administrations of the covenant of grace. It is not included in Murray's 4 volume *Collected Writings*.

The Main Points of the Covenant of Grace — Klaas Schilder.

This was a speech delivered in some places in the Netherlands in 1944 and 1945. It is a good summary of Schilder's covenant theology. He emphasizes the dynamic and relational nature of the covenant of grace. It can be found online at www.spindleworks.com

***Covenant and Election*, J. Van Genderen (Neerlandia: Inheritance Publications, 1995).**
This is a helpful overview of the history of this topic. The author also outlines the similarities and differences between covenant and election.

***Teaching and Preaching the Word: Studies in Dogmatics and Homiletics*, Nicolaas H. Gootjes (Winnipeg: Premier, 2010).**
In terms of covenant theology, especially noteworthy are chapters 4 (Christ's Obedience and Covenant Obedience), chapter 8 (Sign and Seal), chapter 9 (The Promises of Baptism) and chapter 17 (Can Parents Be Sure? Background and Meaning of Canons of Dort, I, 17).

***Reformed Dogmatics*, Herman Bavinck (Grand Rapids: Baker, 2006).**
Bavinck was always a careful theologian who developed his conclusions from a meticulous exegesis of Scripture. He discusses the covenant of grace in volume 3 and he is worthy of close study. In volume 2, he also has a notable discussion of the covenant of works.

***An Everlasting Covenant*, J. Kamphuis (Launceston: Publication Organisation of the Free Reformed Churches of Australia, 1985).**
This is a more technical work which traces some of the finer details in the debates over covenant theology leading up to the Liberation of 1944.

***Covenant, Justification, and Pastoral Ministry*, ed. R. Scott Clark (Phillipsburg: P & R, 2007).**
This is a collection of essays by the faculty of Westminster Seminary California. While there are some important cautionary notes sounded in this volume against the false teachings of Federal Vision theology, the discussion of the theology of Klaas Schilder (especially in chapter 12) is not helpful or fair.

A Puritan Theology: Doctrine for Life, **Joel R. Beeke & Mark Jones (Grand Rapids: Reformation Heritage Books, 2012).**

This important volume contains several chapters on covenant theology. Chapter 19, "The Puritans on Covenant Conditions" is particularly helpful, especially in explaining the distinction between antecedent and consequent conditions.

www.ingramcontent.com/pod-product-compliance
Lightning Source LLC
LaVergne TN
LVHW010745131224
798955LV00028B/941